C000244956

AROUND
MELKSHAM
IN OLD PHOTOGRAPHS

AROUND
MELKSHAM
IN OLD PHOTOGRAPHS

COLLECTED BY

THE MELKSHAM AND DISTRICT
HISTORICAL ASSOCIATION

EDITED BY

KEN MERRETT

ALAN SUTTON
1989

Alan Sutton Publishing
Gloucester

First published 1989

British Library Cataloguing in Publication Data

Melksham in old photographs.
1. Wiltshire. Melksham, history
I. Melksham Historical Association
942.3′15

ISBN 0-86299-670-8

Typesetting and origination by
Alan Sutton Publishing
Printed in Great Britain by
Dotesios Printers Limited

INTRODUCTION

Melksham is a flourishing country and industrial town situated south-east of the Cotswold Hills, lying on the broad clay plain of north-west Wiltshire, in the lovely Avon Vale. The river flows to the Bristol Channel north to south through the town, a place of considerable antiquity. It gave its name to a hundred before the Norman Conquest, also to a royal manor and forest and later to a spa.

The earliest trace of ancient man in Melksham was a polished stone axe of the Neolithic or Bronze Age, found under the roots of a fallen tree before 1916. The Bristol Museum acquired this, but it was destroyed as a result of enemy action in 1940. Another find was a pagan burial 'near the Grove'.

After the invasion of the West Saxons and the gradual rise of the kingdom of Wessex, the community of Melksham was founded, encouraged by the fact that the river could be forded there. At some time during the Saxon period Melksham probably acquired its name, the Old English 'Meolcham'. It was probably a kind of dairy farm settlement, for 'Meolc' is the Old English for milk and 'ham' signifies a settled community, or it could mean an enclosure of dwellings by water meadows. The Saxon kings had a court at nearby Chippenham.

The Domesday survey of 1086 gives the earliest written picture of Melksham, as a thriving community of several hundred people. The Earl Harold mentioned in the Domesday book – King Harold II (Godwinson) – only held the manor a few months. The early Norman kings came to Melksham and between 1200 and 1212 King John visited his manor no fewer than 11 times. In 1257 Henry III gave the hundred and manor to Amice, Countess of Devon, for life, with reversion to Amesbury Priory, a favourite house of the royal family of that time. This Benedictine nunnery dated back to Saxon times, but had been refounded by Henry II. For around 258 years, from approximately 1281 to 1539, when the religious houses were dissolved by King Henry VIII, Amesbury Priory held the hundred and manor of Melksham, and the prioress was the lady of the manor of Melksham. The manor, one of their most valuable properties, was administered by the priory officials. They bought and sold, and took back quantities of produce and livestock to Amesbury. In 1236 the Dean and Chapter of Salisbury were given 20 good oaks from Melksham Forest for making the stalls in Salisbury Cathedral.

In 1541 the manor was granted to Sir Thomas Seymour who sold it immediately in June 1541 to Henry Brouncker of Melksham, a wealthy clothier. He also, in 1548, took up a 99 year lease of the Manor of Melksham Canonhold. He built a manor house on the west side of the Market Place in around 1550, and for the first time the town had a resident lord of the manor, and not just a steward from Amesbury.

From 1671 the lordship of the manor descended in the Long family of Whaddon. However, Place House or Court House, as the manor house was called, was bought in 1657 by Isaac Selfe the younger, whose father lived in the fifteenth-century manor house of Beanacre. Place House remained in this family until 1757, passing by marriage to Richard Jenkyns, and in 1806 to the Heathcotes of Shaw Hill. Later, the manufacturer Mr Charles Maggs purchased it and lived there with his family. They had a rope walk at the rear of the house. His executors sold it to Mr R.L. Lopes for £1,000 on 23 February 1864. Mr Lopes demolished the house. The site, gardens and orchards – more than two acres – were divided into building plots and sold by public auction at the King's Arms on 11 April 1864. A short private road was made and the houses, which still remain today, were erected.

From Saxon times until 1624 when the deforestation was legally completed, Melksham was part of a royal hunting forest. The Saxon kings hunted there, but it was the Norman kings who enclosed larger tracts of wasteland, not only for the sport, venison and game, but for the advantages of timber, and the value of letting off portions for cultivation as arable, meadow, pasture or pannage. The last time stags were reported running in the streets of the town was in 1609, when a number of inhabitants were prosecuted for 'stealing them'.

From the mid-fourteenth century (the time of Edward III) the forest laws and institutions slowly began to languish. Bounds had been reduced and were reduced still more. In 1624 King James I's commissioners enabled the old forest laws to be rescinded. Landowners bought large tracts of what was left. Some of the inhabitants of Melksham who had enjoyed common of pasture and other rights in the forest for generations were upset to find that land they had almost considered their own, now had to be bought outright, or a fine paid and a lease taken up.

Information about the thirteenth-century farming of Melksham Manor survives. Berryfield was one of the common fields for tenants engaged in the old open field farming, which went on for generations. The Conigre field was the manor rabbit warren. It is not certain when mixed farming gave way to almost universal dairy farming. Alongside agriculture went all the manifold kindred trades; maltsters to millers, blacksmiths to tanners – Melksham had them all.

The first documentary evidence of Melksham weavers is in an Assize Roll of 1349; and of fulling mills, in 1555, sited north of the river bridge; however, they must have been there earlier. White broadcloth was the chief manufacture. This English product was appreciated as far away as central Europe. Then there were semi-independent spinners and weavers who obtained the wool and yarn, and worked it all up at home, selling the finished or partly finished cloth for the best offer and not always back to the member of the trade from whom it had come. Later broadcloth had to give way to coloured cloth, which involved dyeing and all the necessary apparatus. Melksham took much longer than some of the bigger wool towns to pick up under the difficulties of the change-over. Some of the weavers lived at the end of the town across the river in or near The City, an old settlement.

The trade was always sensitive to wars at home or abroad. The Civil War which started in the autumn of 1642 was a severe jolt, and many weavers and others involved were partly unemployed. Melksham was never involved in the battles, though the greatest fought in Wiltshire, the Battle of Roundway Down in July 1643, took place only a few miles away. At Lacock Abbey there was a royal garrison. The Parliamentary garrison at Great Chalfield Manor taxed and levied the hundred for money and food.

The trade revived under the Commonwealth and under the Restoration of the Monarchy. As the eighteenth century proceeded there came increasing competition, especially from the Yorkshire woollen industry. The quality was as good as ever, but demands for products did not increase, and the idea of making cheaper products did not appeal. Clothiers and weavers were up against a problem, and there is much to say for both sides. Melksham had several nasty wage riots. That of 1738 was bad; weavers, shearmen and boys were involved, and it went on for nearly a week until the military were called in. Henry Coulthurst who had a weaving factory in the town had his looms, fulling mill and private house wrecked. Later several clothiers went bankrupt. The financial crisis of the 1840s further crippled the trade, but some clothiers survived by their use of new methods, mechanization, and increased efficiency. In the 1790s there were 14 clothiers in the town. Then in the 1850s came the invention of the power loom, which finished cottage weaving for ever. Matravers Mill by the Town Bridge, the last mill to close, survived until 1888.

With the decline of the wool trade in the 1890s a period of industrial development set in which was to reach its high point in the 1960s. In 1889 what is now the Avon Rubber Company moved from Limpley Stoke to the disused cloth mill by the river bridge, and over a century of continuous expansion has played a major role in the industrial and social life of the town. Spencer's Engineering Works had started at the corner of Bath Road and Union Street in 1898 and moved to Beanacre Road in 1903, building up an international reputation in techniques of mechanical handling. The Wilts. United Dairies started by Charles Maggs at West End Farm later moved to New Broughton Road (in 1888). It was the grandfather of this Charles Maggs who transferred his rope-making business to Spa Road in 1803. With the introduction of the steel hawser, rope-making declined and Charles Maggs changed to coir fibre matting and kindred products. Sawtells in Old Broughton Road, established in 1892 as a straw dealing establishment, changed in 1902 to the cleaning of feathers for commercial use and later to mattress and pillow products. Messrs Hurn Bros. started a timber mill in 1854 by the railway station, moving to the Ark site early this century, becoming the largest manufacturer of trellis work in the country. The Wiltshire Farmers moved to Melksham from Atworth where it had started in 1916 and the Co-operative Society established a large creamery opposite the railway station in 1920.

Now, in 1989, another phase declines and only the Avon Rubber Company, still expanding with worldwide ramifications, and Wiltshire Farmers, now West of England Farmers, remain. New industries are evolving on industrial estates on the town perimeter while the old factory sites are taken over for housing development. The town continues as a thriving community with an expanding population and a growing awareness of its potential as a tourist centre. The small market town is increasingly seen as the ideal place to live, without the anonymity and loneliness of the city or the isolation of the village, but with the facilities of the former and the community sense of the latter.

The Avenue, West End, Melksham.

A FIELD BETWEEN KING STREET AND THE CANAL known as 'Potterns' and once leased by Mr E. Bolwell who lived at the Wharf. Later it was bought by the West Wilts. Land and Building Co., to build the West End Estate – Kimber Street and West End – largely under the direction of Mr Oliver Kimber who was the surveyor of the Melksham Local Board in 1889. St Anthony of Padua's Roman Catholic Church was built on the site in 1939. A travelling farmer is recorded as hiring the field on the right to exhibit his performing cow. The cow died and was buried nearby.

DRINKWATER HOUSE, SEMINGTON ROAD. In its heyday this was the home of Job Lewington who was a barge owner and ran a successful business conveying goods to all parts of the country. The gardens ran down to the canal at the rear and included the land on which Western Terrace now stands – a terrace of red brick houses next to the police station. The house was renovated in the 1960s and converted into flats.

THIS IS THE KING STREET TOLL-HOUSE — one of seven on the approaches to the town, of which three are still intact. The last turnpike keeper at King Street was Abram Bolland. He was an old soldier and a veteran of the Indian Mutiny. For lack of alternative transport he had to walk to Trowbridge every week to collect his pension.

KING STREET in the 1900s. On the right a double-fronted shop which was then, as now, a greengrocer's. To the left is a baker's shop kept by a Joseph Sheppard who was said to be a relative of the notorious highwayman, Jack Sheppard. This shop now sells pet foods. In the 1870s it was a kindergarten school run by a Miss Sheppard. Next along can be seen a small grocery business and then comes the entrance to The White Hart; the framework for the sign board can be seen.

CLEVERLY BROS. CYCLE SHOP in the Market Place. It is now an estate agent's premises.

THE WHITE HART HOTEL PREMISES in King Street referred to on the opposite page. Now used as a part of the Samovar premises. The entrance from the main road in the centre was filled in to extend the Samovar shop front. The hotel closed in 1896.

TWO PICTURES showing a row of eighteenth-century cottages now demolished to give access to Thornbank. The smithy on the right was the last working one in the town – run by Mr Petty – and is now incorporated as a room in the house. The sixteenth-century ceiling of the smithy was listed as being of special architectural interest in the 1950s. It is possible that this forge was owned by the Countess of Amesbury. The forge closed in 1939.

A VERY OLD PICTURE of the junction of King Street and the Market Place. On the right is the bow-fronted shop which is prominent in all photographs of the Market Place. In 1900 it was a bootmaker's shop kept by a John Townsend. He had it painted red and, not unreasonably, called it the Red House.

A LATER VIEW of the same site. In the eighteenth and nineteenth centuries this was the site of a guard house to which a man named Southernwood was committed in 1782 'being sworn by a Melksham woman as the father of a child she was expecting'. Some Dragoon Guards had taken over the guard house to store ammunition but, despite protests from the Quartermaster, the constable locked up the man. Southernwood blew the guard house up by striking his knife against some flint and setting light to the ammunition – the building was completely demolished. The man survived, but with horrible burns and one leg so crushed that it had to be amputated.

AN OLD PRINT OF THE MARKET PLACE prior to the demolition of Place House in 1864.

THE MARKET PLACE in around 1870. The Crown Inn built in 1877 took the place of the inn shown in the photograph and was called the Old Crown because there was also an inn called the New Crown (sited next door to Currys towards the Market Place). The low building to the right of the picture was a saddle and harness maker's and was replaced in 1899 by a multiple grocer's building which still stands today. The King's Arms Hotel on the left was a well-known coaching inn and once a popular rendezvous with the hunting fraternity. The Royal Mail left the King's Arms daily for Exeter at 5.30 a.m. and for London at 10.30 a.m. and 8.30 p.m. Before the setting up of the Local Government Board a deep ditch ran through the Market Place carrying away the town's sewage. A wooden bridge crossed the ditch for the benefit of pedestrians.

THE MARKET PLACE in around 1905, showing many features now lost. The old lock-up-cum-weighbridge to the left and the town pump to the right were both demolished in 1947. The handle of the pump is clearly seen – the spout was low enough for buckets to be filled and an iron cup was hung on a chain for the thirsty traveller. There was a horse trough on the far side from this view point. Many residents well remember being able to drink at this pump in the 1930s. The well is still there under a round cover. The saddler's shop is clearly seen and the gates to Melksham House are in line with building frontages. Note the man in a Wiltshire smock and leggings in front of the old Market Hall. See also the tethering posts and racks, the cobbled pavement, and the material evidence of horse-drawn traffic.

THE TOWN HALL was built in 1847. In the 1880s the arch to the left of the entrance contained a butcher's shop and that on the right housed the town stocks. The last man to be placed in the stocks was named Thomas – a blacksmith from Bathford. He was sentenced to five hours for being drunk and disorderly but 'the stress of the weather induced his merciful release after two hours'. These stocks are presently stored in the Local History Museum at the Rachel Fowler Centre. The two-storey building to the right was used as the police station and the space between housed the fire engine.

THE GERMAN GUN, a souvenir relic of the First World War, was donated to the town. (Trowbridge qualified for a tank!) On a quiet night in 1921, as a protest against lack of employment, a group of citizens manhandled the gun from its site in the Market Place and dumped it in the river by Hurn's Saw Mills. One of the group responsible for this dastardly deed still walks the streets of the town – a free man! The gun was recovered and replaced in the Market Place until used for scrap in the Second World War.

MARKET DAY IN MELKSHAM. In the nineteenth century the Tuesday market was held fortnightly to alternate with Trowbridge market. The highlight of each year used to be the Melksham Fair held in the Market Place on 27 and 28 July. The first day was devoted to the sale of cattle, pigs, sheep and horses and the second day to amusements. The sales pitch for horses extended from the Market Place to the turnpike along King Street, cattle from Place Road to the Crown Inn and up Spa Road to the Canal Bridge. Sheep were penned in the High Street and Church Street and in Bank Street as far as the Reading Rooms. Pigs were sold in the Market and in Lowbourne. The Congregational Sunday School held its annual outing on the second day of the fair to offer the children more improving entertainment and in 1910 the fair was closed by an Act of Parliament on the grounds that it brought too many undesirables into the town.

IN THE MARKET PLACE next to the entrance to Melksham House stood Mattingly's, a firm of saddlers. Previously it had been a shop selling only bread and occupied by a Mr Barton. In 1899 the International Stores was built on this site. The group at the entrance includes the manager, Mr Frank Hiscocks.

THE JUNCTION OF MARKET PLACE with Spa Road. Note the lovely old buildings, one with pillared entrance; all of these have now been demolished to make way for the shops which stand there today.

AN EXTENDED VIEW of the shops with the addition of the New Hall built in 1877 by the generosity of Miss Rachel Fowler. Up to 1939 the Hall was used for various public functions. Before the New Hall was built, the site was occupied by a jeweller's shop kept by a Mr Bullock. In 1951 grandfather clocks bearing the name Bullock were in use in the Town Hall, Lloyds Bank and A.G. Smith & Son. Next to the New Hall stood an attractive house known as The Cabin. In 1880 this was the home of Mr T. Matravers who was prominent in the cloth industry. The house can still be seen behind the façade built for the public house. Between times The Cabin was used as the Labour Club and later on as the local branch of the County Library.

THE CROWN INN decorated for the Coronation of Queen Elizabeth. The previous building included a club room on the first floor which could be approached only from a stairway which covered the width of the pavement. Pedestrians would have to step into the road to get round this.

Place House, Melksham. Demolished in 1863. Publ. by A. W. Jolliffe & Cᵒ. Melksham. Wilkinson's Series.

PLACE HOUSE – the great manor house built by Henry Brouncker in around 1550. The site and gardens were divided into building plots and sold by public auction at the King's Arms on 11 April 1864. A short private road was made and the houses erected which still remain today. Note the town police officer, second from the left.

CLARE HOUSE, built after the demolition of Place House. The wall abutting the pavement was built with stones from Place House. Note the monkey puzzle tree which was for years a feature of the Market Place.

THE ENTRANCES TO MELKSHAM HOUSE and the Assembly Hall prior to 1950, when the archway to the Assembly Hall was demolished, and the entrance gates to Melksham House set back to their present site and the walls behind the pillars demolished.

THE LIMES, once known as Brunswick House, so named probably in honour of the marriage of the Prince of Wales (later George IV) to Caroline of Brunswick in 1795. It was last occupied as a dwelling house by Dr William Keir and later by his son Dr Ivan Keir. It was eventually taken over by Stringer's Garage and is now a watersports shop.

AN AMERICAN ARMY UNIT parked in the Market Place in 1914.

THE RACHEL FOWLER CENTRE. This was formerly a Congregational Church built in 1788 and closed following a union with the Methodist Church. The entrance lobby shown in the photograph was enlarged in the 1920s. It was designed by Sir George Oatley, a Melksham man, who also designed Bristol University. In 1979 the building was acquired by a group of residents in the town who formed the Melksham & District Arts Association and it is now a thriving centre of the cultural and social life of the town.

THE TWO COTTAGES on the right of the approach to the church once functioned as a turnpike gate. At one time an occupant, a well-known local character, was said to have set off along the canal towpath one morning with the avowed intent of stopping the American Civil War.

THIS PICTURE dates from around 1910. Note the four gate pillars to Place Road, the tethering posts and the premises of the Wilts. & Dorset Bank, subsequently taken over by Lloyds Bank together with the Capital & Counties Bank. Place House had been unoccupied for several years prior to its demolition and the gardens had been taken over by Maggs for rope manufacture and a rope walk extended right back to the church boundary. When Place House was sold, the rope walk was transferred to a site in Spa Road where ropes could be woven in lengths of up to three quarters of a mile.

THE ENTRANCE TO THE KING'S ARMS courtyard and stables and, on the left, H. Bailey & Co., Cycle and Motor Agents. Bransons later took over the site and then Phillips & Whittaker who installed petrol pumps on the pavement. With increasing traffic the site became insufferable as a garage and it is now an extension to the bar facilities of the King's Arms.

FOUR VIEWS OF THE HIGH STREET before 1910. Note the shop awnings out to the edge of the street – a feature of Edwardian England and a predecessor of the drop roller blinds of today. The trees in the distance to the left of the street were two limes from which a house called Lindens derived its name. This house was demolished to make way for the cinema which opened in 1912 and in 1964 was demolished to make room for a shopping precinct. Next to the bank on the left stood a chemist's shop, run in 1878 by a Mr Laine, then by a Mr Bush, followed by Mr Hughes, and then by Boots. It is now a building society's office. Next door in the 1880s was Gowens Drapers, still trading under the same name. On the right, next to the Wesleyan Church, was the residence of Mr Awdry, a solicitor, who as Captain of the old Volunteers played a leading part in the Bear Hotel riots in 1865.

THE NEW CROWN INN in the High Street stood next door to what is now Currys. Next to the inn lived Mr W. Lewington, a tailor. A contemporary tells how Mr Lewington held a sale of obsolete bowler hats at 6*d*. each in various styles from the previous 30 years.

THE NEW CROWN INN has given way to Mr Hutton's butchers shop. The girl with the hoop will be remembered by older residents as Mrs W.T. Richards whose husband ran a scrap metal merchant's business at Westleigh House, King Street.

HUTTON'S BUTCHERS SHOP has been replaced by Mr Pocock's electricians store, and what was Mr Lewington tailor's shop is by now Brewer's bakers. Note the post office is on the left.

A WIDER VIEW of No. 37. The entrance to Watson's Court and, to the right, the home and offices of Mr Justly Awdry, a solicitor who was also Captain of the old Volunteers and who in that capacity was criticized for his handling of the hustings' riots round the Bear Hotel in 1865. Note the inn sign of the Royal Oak to the far left of the picture.

PART OF MR AWDRY'S HOUSE has been converted for Mr Gowing's grocery shop. This was a very high class establishment with chairs at the counter for the customers convenience while giving their orders.

THE CONVERSION of Mr Awdry's fine old Georgian house to commerce is complete with the advent of yet another building society and estate agent's office. Mr Gowing's splendid store has given way to the opticians.

THIS SHOP on the corner at the junction of High Street and Church Street is now a jeweller's business, but in the 1950s was an ironmonger's run by L.J. Bigwood. Earlier it was a motor and motor cycle repair shop. The existing building was constructed after the complete demolition of the one shown in the picture.

THE HIGH STREET in around 1920. The shop on the left, at the junction with Church Street – now a jeweller's – was previously a hardware business catering for repairs to motor cycles and motor cars. The building opposite, adorned by a magnificent pear espalier, is Stratton, Sons & Mead's wholesale grocers, now Woolworths. Next can just be seen an arched passageway which is now a baker's shop. In the middle distance is the George Inn – now the site of the British Gas showrooms.

A SIMILAR VIEW to that above, taken about ten years later. The house next to Stratton's has been demolished, the pear tree cut down and an annexe built on to Stratton's to provide office accommodation. Two telegraph boys (a vanished tribe) stand in front of the car.

ANOTHER VIEW OF THE HIGH STREET in the 1920s. Note the fine old cedar behind Bank House.

STRATTON, SONS & MEAD'S was a flourishing wholesale grocery business established by James Stratton in around 1842. He lived at The Grange in the Conigre, later over the shop, and he finally moved with three of his daughters, Mary, Maria and Caroline, to Leaze Cottage. The business was carried on by two of his sons, Alfred and George. For nearly 100 years the Stratton family was to play a dominant role in the religious and political life of the town.

A VIEW OF THE HIGH STREET C. 1910. The lime trees are in full leaf. The two dwellings on the left are now a public house, once known as The Board and affectionately known to its patrons as the Parson's Nose, which it has now been officially renamed. Curiously, a local man recalled that in his youth in the late 1800s one of the houses was known as Clergy House. The shop on the corner of Church Street, D.J. Hiam's, was once a baker's and then a fishmonger's before being taken over by W.H. Smith & Sons. In earlier times it was the site of some stables.

POULSOM'S BUTCHERS SHOP in around 1900, standing on the site now occupied by Martin's Newsagents. Mr Poulsom transferred his business across the road to its present position in the early 1920s.

NOW OCCUPIED BY CURRYS. This picture dates from 1910. Mr Jolliffe ran the post office together with a stationery shop and most of the pictures which we have of old Melksham are from postcards produced and sold by him. Before him a Mr Cochrane ran a similar business. Eventually the post office took over the entire premises including the Royal Oak before moving to a new site in Church Street.

ANOTHER VIEW OF THE HIGH STREET dated around 1910. Note the state of the road, the absence of traffic and the small number of shoppers.

Top, left.
HENRY WHITE LTD, drapers and men's outfitters on the site now occupied by Boots in the High Street. At the time of this photograph the town's manually operated telephone exchange was run on the first floor above the shop. A list of tradesmen in the mid-1800s makes interesting reading. There were five bakers, fourteen boot and shoemakers, six butchers, seven drapers, one greengrocer only, thirteen grocers, four leather sellers, two saddle and harness makers, two straw hat makers and five tailors. The population of Melksham in 1840 was 5,896. In 1793 it had been 5,026 at which time Swindon was a small village of 1,198! A complete list of tradesmen in 1940 includes no building society or estate agent offices. Nor does it include a fishmonger. It is reported that in Trowbridge in 1819 – 'there was not a fish, poultry or game sold in the town' and when Parson Crabbe wished to give a party he would have to send to Bath for the things he required.

Bottom, left.
A WET CARNIVAL PROCESSION in the 1920s. An extension of the view down the High Street in the previous picture. The buildings beyond the third Union Jack (top left) were demolished for the precinct. A mention of tradespeople calls to mind other ways of earning a living. John Gunning of Church Street collected canal water in an 18 gallon barrel mounted on wheels. He would push this around the town selling the water at 1*d*. a bucket. John Gunning supported a widowed mother and an imbecile brother and was one of the casualties of the Bear Hotel riots in 1865, although he was no more than an innocent bystander. Another town character would follow the London coach as far as Devizes, somersaulting and performing other physical contortions for the amusement of the passengers in expectation of tips. He would wait for the returning coach in the evening and perform again on the way back to Melksham.

THE SHOP ON THE LEFT, when vacated by Poulsoms in 1922, was opened as a café. The next shop along, once Butt's tailors establishment, is here seen as Sawyer's greengrocer's. These buildings were demolished in favour of the precinct.

A VIEW OF THE HIGH STREET looking south and taken before Sawyer's greengrocers had moved to the other side of the cinema. The two linden trees in front of the cinema have long since disappeared.

SHOPS IN THE HIGH STREET in the 1890s. On the left is Simpson's, ironmongers (now a café) and next door is Mrs Jones', drapers shop (now Poulsom's). On the right is the entrance (now filled) to an alley-way leading to the rear and accommodating Brewer's bakery shop.

MRS JONES' SHOP is now a grocery shop by 1900. It was later to become a café owned by a Mr Gill before he did an exchange with Mr Poulsom in 1920s. The little boy will be known to many older residents as Mr Frank Gill, for many years associated with the British Legion.

THE PICTURE HALL — later called Maxime Cinema — was opened in November 1912 by the High Sheriff of Wiltshire. It had seating for 550 patrons. It closed in 1964 to make room for the Avon Shopping Precinct. The two lime trees were for many years a feature of the High Street. Before the cinema was built these trees marked the entrance to Linden House, the residence of Mr Flooks.

THE FOYER OF THE PICTURE HALL. A most extraordinary room in which are seen a Greek statue beneath a massive ox head, a stag's head and old armour and firearms suspended everywhere. The furniture and radiators are of ornate Edwardian style, yet by contrast the light fittings are of a restrained geometric style.

NO. 1 BANK STREET (now Gompel's Chemists). One of the linden trees is on the left and behind can be seen part of Linden House. A new building has been built on land at the entrance to Linden House. This house was the residence of Miss Fowler. She was a Quaker who, amongst other gifts, gave the town the New Hall and the Retreat Almshouses. It was reported that such was the respect held for Miss Fowler that when her funeral cortège arrived at the Friends' Meeting House in King Street where she was to be buried, the rear of the procession was still forming up in Bank Street. A nephew of Miss Fowler – Sir Robert Fowler – was twice Lord Mayor of London, and a brother invented the famous Fowler steam plough.

THE START OF BANK STREET, so called after the Capital and Counties Bank which is just visible on the right. This was demolished in 1960. The picture was taken probably in 1920 and the series of steps for mounting the high pavement can be seen. They were removed during the Second World War because of danger in the blackout.

A CLEAR VIEW OF BANK STREET at the turn of the century. Note on the right hand side there is no kerb to the footpath in front of what is now the Liberal Club and was then the entrance to a slaughter house. On the corner of Union Street is an imposing building which was demolished in the 1920s to provide the forecourt for the little shop which was for many years Riddick's newsagents. The bridge and the access to the ford are clearly visible. On the left hand side, note the steps to the high pavement and Smith, the draper's. This little shop was in the ownership of the same man from 1850 to 1906.

THE SAME PREMISES as in the previous picture, but taken in 1910 with a display of Christmas trees and poultry. The delivery handcart on the left is interesting and was a common sight prior to 1939.

TWO PICTURES of the Roberts brothers' grocery and pork butchers shop. The first is dated around 1920 and the second 1928. In 1954 these brothers were still running the business and were by then very senior citizens. In the 1930s they ran their own slaughterhouse in Church Street. George E. Day's tailors shop can be seen in the second picture with The Grapes inn beyond it.

A VIEW OF BANK STREET in the 1950s. On the left are the Reading Rooms, built in 1852. In 1863 these were used by the Mutual Improvement Society which, among other activities, organized 'penny readings' for those unable to read. On 19 December 1863 the readings were given by the Reverend Badham, J.H. Gwatkin, E. Styles and H. Matravers. Those attending paid 1*d.* admission and on that particular evening the room was 'crowded to excess' to hear readings from contemporary authors, with Dickens in great demand.

TWO SEMI-DETACHED HOUSES were built on this site, formerly sheds used by the Wilts. Sack Hiring Co. The houses are here seen in the process of demolition. These demolitions were also to include the old Bank House, the home of the old Capital and Counties Bank, and the George Inn. A field at the rear of the Reading Rooms was presented to the town by Mr George White of Whitley, a cheesemonger, as a site for a new Cottage Hospital; this was opened in 1895 and eventually closed after the Second World War. The building now houses the Labour Club.

A VIEW OF BATH ROAD c. 1876. The Bear Hotel is on the left with the stables beyond and then the wall of the gardens of Ark House. The stone steps were a feature along the length of the high pavement in Bank Street, but were removed during the last war, being a danger to the public during the blackout. In the distance is the river bridge.

BANK STREET from outside the Bear Hotel in around 1910. The Liberal Club is not yet built and the forecourt of the shop at the junction with Union Street is not yet visible. Coaches to Bath and Bristol and to London left the Bear Hotel daily. In addition, in the 1890s, Mrs Mary Adams with her two sons, who ran the inn, maintained carriage and horses for hire with postilions elaborately dressed in buckskin trousers with red or blue jackets, whichever was preferred by the hirer. Stabling was available for 50 horses. On the middle left are the Reading Rooms built in 1852.

THIS HOUSE stood at the junction of Church Walk and Bank Street. It was purchased for £505 by the Baptist Church in 1887 for use as a manse and was sold for £800 in 1904. Subsequently it became the home of the Berry family who played a prominent part in the town's affairs. The house was replaced by the one formerly associated with Mr Anderson Vowles, a dental surgeon, and it is now occupied by Mr Wisbey.

A VIEW OF BANK STREET facing north after the Liberal Club had been built.

A VIEW OF THE HIGH STREET with Woolworths under construction.

THE OLD GEORGE INN with Bank House beyond.

BATH ROAD in January 1926. The gas showrooms are now the Seafood Restaurant. The manager of the town's gasworks lived in the house next door. Behind these buildings was the original site of Spencer's Engineering factory, trading as Spencer & Gillett. Metal pillars bearing that name are still visible in the Town Hall. A story is told of one Abel Curnick who stood watching the workmen excavate the foundations for the second gasometer. One of the workmen called 'Come on down, Abel' to which Abel replied, 'No, 'tis too high down for I'. The flooding of the main street was an annual hazard and usually extended from Union Street to the Bell Inn. It was reported that one year two trees were floated from the sawyers yard (No. 79) into the Bear Hotel yard opposite.

SIX

Warminster and d

Cautious council

A CAGEY response to a request for money over the next three years was given by Corsley parish council on Monday night.

The National Association for Local Councils wants to raise £750,000 by 1994, so that it can buy its own premises in London.

At the moment, NALC is affected by spiralling rent costs for it offices in Great Russell Street.

Before deciding whether to contribute half a per cent of its annual £2,500 budget (£12,50) for three years, Corsley is seeking more information from the Wiltshire branch.

Councillors questioned the need for an office in the centre of London; the value of membership, and Mr John White wondered

Cors exte

CORSLEY parish lors gave a firm plans to again exte village's Birchwood into an adjoining fie

Before them was put forward by M. (Builders) Ltd of Fro area is just under tw and is owned by the which has built and 'executive' homes in th sac since 1986.

"This is a special area. It would be a bul settlement. It's over the residential development a be out of scale and harm the existing area of Heath," said chairman an councillor, Cmdr. Robin C

"It is totally unacceptal Other councillors agr there were plenty of ho

A CARNIVAL PROCESSION moving along Bath Road, probably in 1922. The yard behind the wall was the local council depot and on this site is a row of red brick shops. At the beginning of the century, before the council took the site, there was a sawyer's yard here. The boys in the farm cart were said to be from Monkton Combe School and returning from a cricket match. Carnival pictures taken from this angle were by Mr W. Riddick, newsagent and local photographer, who took them from his upstairs window. He subsequently moved his business to the corner of Union Street.

THE APPROACH to the King George V Playing Field from Bath Road. The shop and garage on the left were cleared to facilitate the entrance to the Gateway Supermarket. Queen Mary Garden is behind the wall on the right.

THE ENTRANCE to the Avon Rubber Co. offices. The toilets on the right were demolished in the 1960s to improve the entrance and exit to the Avon car park.

STANDING ON THE BRIDGE, facing north. The houses on the right, known as Ark Terrace, were mostly demolished to improve the access to Hurn Brother's timber yard.

BATH ROAD, C. 1930. The shop on the left was the Co-op Society's second grocery store in the town and beyond this is Smith Keen's boot and shoe shop. The Co-op store had its own stabling and bakehouse at the rear, with an access from the New Broughton Road.

AN EXTENSION of the previous photograph. Next to Smith Keen's shop came a house occupied by the gardener employed at the Island, then the Willow Temperance Hotel and Café. The passage way beyond led to a row of three cottages set at right angles to the road. It would seem that the Willow Café was, in 1875, used as a coffee tavern and was opened in that year by Canon Warre. Clergy of the town held vouchers to give to the 'deserving poor' to obtain sustenance as an alternative to giving cash which would probably have been spent on alcoholic drinks.

NEXT TO THE WILLOW CAFÉ a small shop beyond the gangway (No. 84) has given way to J.G. Boddington's barbers shop.

NEXT TO BODDINGTON'S came a pair of early Georgian houses, each with a flight of steps and curved handrails. In the 1930s Mrs Ward ran a fish and chip dispensary in the house shown here. Both houses were demolished in the late 1940s because they were declared unsafe.

A VIEW OF THE MISSION ROOM in Bath Road on the site of the Avon Rubber Co. visitors' car park. The earliest records suggest that it was a carpenter's shop used by a Jim Hurn, who lived opposite in what was later the Willow Café. His sons, Walter and Albert, developed the business and later moved it to the site of Ark House – Hurn Brothers. In the earlier days the Mission Rooms were used for various functions not specifically religious and the origin of the title 'Mission' is not clear.

BATH ROAD UNDER FLOOD sometime before 1914. The buildings behind the horse and waggon were demolished to make way for the Avon Rubber Co.'s canteen and works entrance. Note one of the town's many blacksmith's forges to the right.

THE ONLY ENTRANCE to the Avon works before 1930 was at the right of the front offices. The rapid expansion of the works could only be towards Beanacre Road and what had formerly been a builder's yard was acquired to give improved access. The canteen was to be built later during the Second World War on the left, and the cottages on the right made way for the personnel department building.

THERE IS A REFERENCE TO A BRIDGE at Melksham in 1300. The bridge in 1637 was in such a bad state that in April of that year the Quarter Sessions ordered the townspeople to repair it by November subject to a penalty of a £40 fine. Today's bridge was built in 1814 to replace the old one which had been destroyed by flood water. The river was fordable at this point, to the north of the bridge, and the ford was still in use within living memory of the townsfolk. Up to 1928 there was only one footpath on the bridge, but it was widened in 1928/9 to provide one on the north side.

THREE COTTAGES and a shop standing next to the Mission Room (above and below), demolished in 1966 to make way for the Avon Rubber Co.'s visitors' car park. Before the demolition Mr Hunt ran a butcher's business in the shop.

FOOD DISTRIBUTION during the First World War. The site in Church Street will be remembered by older inhabitants as Fred Park's fishmongers.

IT IS DIFFICULT TO IMAGINE a cottage with roses around the door so close to the town centre, but these cottages with their paling fences stood immediately next to Edmund's shop in Church Street. They were demolished to make way for the Co-op furniture store, now The Spree shopping centre.

CHURCH STREET in around 1914. Note the cottages adjoining the last shop on the right (seen in close up in the previous view). On the extreme right is a hydrant with a curved arm, to reach into the horse-drawn water cart used to damp down the dusty roads. The row of houses (left centre) was known as Victory Terrace. Which victory is not known. In the late 1920s approximately 70 people lived in Church Street. In 1989 there are only four.

A CLOSE UP OF MR HILL'S BUTCHERS SHOP referred to in the previous caption. It was not unusual to leave the display of meat and poultry outside overnight, albeit with some supervision.

NEXT TO MR HILL'S came a sweet shop kept by Mrs Maslen and her son George. Although George was deformed, he was an excellent kite flyer and had the additional distinction of being the first to introduce fried chipped potatoes into the town. He sold them from a handtruck which he pushed around the town. The site was recently Mortimer's greengrocers and is now a building society office.

THE PRESENT VIEW of the shops. The cottages have given way to The Spree shopping centre. R.J. Edmunds' premises are much as before, but the two small shops are now a building society office.

SHEEP purchased at the market on their way to Mr Hill's slaughterhouse. There were three slaughterhouses in Church Street at this time in the early 1930s: Mr Hill's, at the rear of what is now Pearce's Furnishings; Messrs Roberts of Bank Street where Mr Bewley has his Chapel of Rest; Messrs Norris and Archards where Chaloner Walk has been built. The latter two were solely for pig killing.

THE ROUND HOUSE, a relic of the cloth industry, dating from the eighteenth century, has had many uses over the years since the cloth industry went into decline. Up to then it had been used as a drying house. It was at some time the armoury for the local Rifle Volunteers who had their Drill Hall opposite, then a store for the corn dealers and now in 1989 it is the Tourist Information Centre.

BETWEEN THE WARS the Co-operative movement flourished in Melksham sufficiently to support two large grocery establishments. The one in Church Street is now Pearce's Furnishings. The second one was by the Town Bridge.

COTTAGES IN CHURCH STREET which were demolished to afford an entrance to the car park. Beyond is the Masonic Hall. A majority might agree that the Conservative Club in Bank Street has the most pleasing frontage in the town, but the nineteenth century Masonic Hall building would find few supporters. It houses the Chaloner Lodge founded by Captain Chaloner, who lived at Melksham House from 1895 to 1903 during which period he was MP for the Westbury Division.

THE FUNERAL of Mr Matthews, retired station master, in the early 1920s. It prompts the thought that funerals today are not what they used to be.

Melksham.

CANON SQUARE before the erection of the War Memorial. The railed-in garden was traditionally said to be a burial place for victims of the plague, a view which is supported by the coffin shape of the enclosure; this shape was retained when the memorial was built. The old Church Rooms were partially demolished when the new vicarage was built. Only the gabled end now remains. The vicarage was rebuilt in the nineteenth century. The Andrews and Dury map of 1773 shows that Church Street continued across the site where the Vicarage now stands and then turned left to give access to the Tithe Barn.

THIS IMPOSING EDIFICE, once known as the Church House, was at one time the residence of the Revd W. Mottram, a Congregational Minister, and subsequently of the station master, Mr Matthews. In the 1950s it was converted into flats before the site was cleared to make way for the new post office, since when it has achieved a veneration it never enjoyed previously.

THE WAR MEMORIAL. In 1919 an influential body of townspeople was in favour of purchasing Melksham House and grounds for development as a public park and recreation ground. However, a series of appeals to the townspeople failed to elicit sufficient interest in this proposal for a memorial. In the meantime the then vicar of Melksham, Canon Wyld, who had lost his only son in the war, approached the relatives of the fallen, who agreed between them to donate £200 towards the cost of building a stone cross in Canon Square. Canon Wyld offered to donate the balance of £150 required. The memorial has therefore the distinction of having been secured by the relatives of those named on the Roll of Honour rather than by the town as a whole.

THIS IS MULBERRY COTTAGE in Church Street as it stands (only just) in 1989 and included here because it is soon to be converted into flats after years of neglect. It was once the home of the influential Redman family and later of the Bigwoods. Its last occupant was Arthur Angell, verger at St Michael's Church and manager of the Labour Exchange office which operated from his front room.

THE INTERIOR of the Parish Church in around 1880. The huge pews were replaced in 1892. The existing fresco over the chancel was not painted until 1921.

THE URBAN DISTRICT COUNCIL'S REFUSE COLLECTION outside No. 11 Canon Square sometime before 1910.

A VIEW of the east end of the Parish Church. The pathway leads to a door in the wall of what was the garden of the large house which stood where today's post office is built. The east wall was built in around 1130. The corner butresses were added in 1450 when the roof of the chancel was raised and the present larger windows inserted.

A PRINT OF THE PARISH CHURCH, before 1845, the date that the tower was moved to the west end of the church. This was part of an extensive restoration carried out by Thomas Wyatt who, because of the mischief which he did to so many churches, became known as 'the destroyer'. This view is taken from the south side of the church.

NOS. 4 & 6 CANON SQUARE in the 1920s. These cottages, together with No. 2, were originally built in the late fifteenth century. During the late eighteenth century the original front wall of the cottages was removed and the new front wall was built in the early Georgian manner. A new roof was then built over the cottages to cover the wider span. The original thatch was taken off and a new roof with a tiled covering was then completed. Whether the existing tiles, which are a glazed Roman tile, were used in the eighteenth century is not known. The west gable wall of Canon House is also of cruck construction. Parts of the north cruck blade remain.

NO. 5 CHURCH WALK. That part forming the centre gable dates from the sixteenth century, extensions to the south and north were added later. Nos. 7 & 9 beyond were once one large house, as were Nos. 16 & 18 opposite.

Melksham.

THE JUNCTION of Lowbourne with the High Street. The double-fronted shop of Flooks & Manning was both a draper's and a wine and spirit shop. It is now the site of the Midland Bank. To the left is a baker's shop belonging, in the early 1900s, to Burgess and later to Wests. This, together with the Co-op furniture store adjacent, was demolished to make way for a supermarket and is now Lloyds chemist shop.

THIS PICTURE OF THE GEORGE INN dated 1898 is virtually a portrait of the family of Mrs W. Cook, the wife of the proprietor. Descendants of the family are still living in the area.

THE DEMOLITION OF THE GEORGE INN caused some dissention at the time, but a traffic bottleneck already existed which would have been insupportable by present times.

THE OLD CLERGY HOUSE is now known as the The Board and is in process of renovation.

ANOTHER 'ROUND HOUSE', a drying room connected with the mill operating in the building on the right. Both are now used as dwelling houses.

TWO VIEWS OF LOWBOURNE. Above is Flooks & Manning's which was later taken over as a furniture store by the Co-operative Society. Below is the same building viewed from the opposite direction, before the building of the supermarket. Bolwell's, stationers and printers premises, prior to 1895 housed the local hospital established in 1868. It had accommodation for four beds for men on the first floor and three beds for women on the second floor.

STILL IN LOWBOURNE and next door to Bolwell's (now the Card Centre) is the butcher's shop run by Mr Elihu Alford. He was said to be the first butcher in Melksham to sell colonial meat. On his death the premises reverted to a dwelling house occupied until 1988 by his daughter, May.

LOWBOURNE in 1910. The trees were part of the grounds of Lowbourne House where the Health Clinic and the Library now stand. The large open door on the left was an entrance to the yard, stables and outhouses of the George Inn. The tall chimney-like pipe on the left was one of a number in the town which took off into the atmosphere any gases which might otherwise dangerously have accumulated in the underground sewers.

A SLIGHTLY EARLIER VIEW of Lowbourne, looking towards Bank Street. The row of Georgian houses on the left was called Lowbourne Place. In the distance is the garden wall of The Lindens, demolished to make way for the cinema.

LOWBOURNE in the 1920s, before it was widened and before the cricket field on the left was acquired by the Urban District Council to mark the Silver Jubilee of King George V.

Sandridge Road, Melksham.

AT THE TOP OF LOWBOURNE HILL at the junction with Sandridge Road and Forest Road. The wall in the centre is the parapet of the bridge over the Wilts. & Berks. Canal, which passed under the road at this point *en route* for Lacock. The hurdles were the recognized protection of roadworks against road users and straying animals.

THE JUNCTION of Bath Road and New Broughton Road in around 1880. The house on the left still stands, but those on the right, together with the chimney of Mr Phillips' dyehouse, gave way to the United Dairies creamery in 1888.

TWO VIEWS of the junction of Bath Road and New Broughton Road, with the old Co-op grocery store now abandoned and soon to be demolished to provide additional parking facilities for Avon workers. The chimney built for the United Dairies has been truncated following the closure of the factory, but happily enough remains to exemplify the art of bricklaying. On the day that the building of the chimney was completed the Conservative Band (affectionately known as the 'thirsty thirteen') played a selection of music from the scaffolding at the top.

THE OTHER END OF NEW BROUGHTON ROAD joining up with the Old Broughton Road.

A BIT OF OLD MELKSHAM
SITE FOR NEW School

THE BAPTIST SUNDAY SCHOOL was housed in a lean-to attached to the church before 1908. Mr E.J. Lee owned the four cottages and he donated this site to the Church for the building of a new school between the church and Broughton Road. This was formally opened on 28 February 1909. It cost £1,802, but this amount was not paid off until June 1916. It was a pity that the new building should obscure the historic church at the rear.

THE BAPTIST CHURCH in the old Broughton Road was licensed in 1784. The church (the people, not the building) dates from 1669. In 1776 there were only ten members. That year the wealthy and influential Ledyard family moved from Rode into Ark House and under this family's leadership the church revived to the point when the present church was built to accommodate the large congregations.

"The City" Melksham.— King John slept at "The Red Lion" after hunting in the neighbouring forest

A CORNER OF MELKSHAM with great character, known as The City, and undoubtedly one of the oldest parts of the town. The Red Lion Inn does not appear so named until the nineteenth century, but tradition has it that King John kept a hunting lodge on this site. All the properties beyond the Red Lion fell into disrepair and, except for one, were demolished in the 1950s. It is probable that the narrow thoroughfare was the main road to Corsham and Bath in medieval times – an extension from the ford across the river just north of the bridge.

THIS ROW OF WEAVERS' COTTAGES, known as Ganes Buildings, ran parallel with the Bath Road between the Old and New Broughton Roads. They were demolished in the 1960s. In the 1980s more strenuous efforts to save them would have been demanded.

OLD BROUGHTON ROAD at the junction with Bath Road. The Red Lion Inn is on the right with the Baptist Church Sunday School beyond.

TWO VIEWS OF OLD BROUGHTON ROAD facing east in the 1950s. The houses on the right above were cleared for the roundabout on the Western Way. The first building on the left was formerly the mineral water factory of A. Coombes & Sons Ltd.

TAKEN FROM THE SAME STANDPOINT as the previous illustration, but facing west along the road to Holt. The first of the two cottages on the left is thought to have been the turnpike house.

THE MELKSHAM ALMSHOUSES, now forming part of the charities known as the Melksham Almshouses Public & Eleemosynary Charities, were initially administered by trustees under a deed of settlement dated 5 May 1864. By this settlement Miss Rachel Fowler transferred five houses and gardens to 12 trustees who, during her life, had to abide by her decision in regard to the persons who were chosen to occupy the almshouses. The settlement set out the rules and regulations on how the trustees were to administer the almshouses after her death. The persons appointed to occupy the houses had to be over 50 years old and had to be widows or spinsters of 'good moral character and also not in receipt of parochial relief', though it was provided that one or two of the houses could be occupied by married couples.

COTTAGES IN OLD BROUGHTON ROAD, demolished in the 1960s, which formed part of the area known as The Gardens, from which the new estate on the opposite side of the road derives its name.

THE JUNCTION of Bath Road and Beanacre Road. This site has been absorbed by the subway and general road improvements. The house to the left of the picture is Knapp House, also demolished for the road changes. The sightseers are probably awaiting a carnival procession. The lady on the extreme right is Mrs Olive Phelps, who is still active in the town today. The date is 1928.

ANOTHER VIEW OF BATH ROAD at the junction with Beanacre Road showing the gradient which was built up to enable the road to the cross the railway line. The railway engineers originally planned a level crossing!

AN AERIAL VIEW of Bath Road and Beanacre Road. The house in the top centre was The Chestnuts, for many years the residence of Mr Henry Sawtell, the son of the founder of the feather factory. Mr Sawtell was a leading figure in the world of greyhound racing and coursing, being Chief Steward of the Greyhound Racing Association. All his dogs bore the prefix 'Melksham' to their names and his leading greyhound 'Melksham Tom' was, in the 1930s, the fastest ever.

A CLOSE UP OF THE CHESTNUTS. In the picture above, the Avon works are encroaching northwards, and they were soon to take over the site of The Chestnuts in an extension up to the Beanacre Road.

THE ATTEMPT TO ESTABLISH A SPA in Melksham was initiated by several respectable gentlemen in 1813. No doubt they were moved by an analysis by Dr Gibbs of Bath who asserted, *inter alia*, that the waters 'act on the bowels gently, safely but decidedly'. Unfortunately, along with similar efforts at Holt and Seend, it could not compete with Bath and declined after 1822. Three elegant houses remain but some new bungalows have been built by the former Pump Room which is now a dwelling.

DOGS BEHAVE DECOROUSLY and patients perambulate in the grounds of the Pump Room. This is a print issued in a brochure advertising the spa.

PART OF CHARLES MAGGS' COIR MATTING FACTORY which was founded in 1803 in what had previously been a cloth mill on the banks of the canal at Spa Road. The business initially was mainly concerned with rope, making lengths of up to a quarter of a mile, but with the advent of the steel hawser, rope-making declined and production was concentrated on coir fibre matting. The site became derelict in the 1950s and was cleared for housing development.

IT WAS THE GRANDSON of the above Charles Maggs who opened a milk collecting depot at the West End Farm in the late nineteenth century. When business expanded to warrant separate office accommodation he built on the site of his matting factory, and it was from this small building that the Wilts. United Dairies was to expand into the national Unigate concern.

THE LEGACY of well preserved houses built by the cloth merchants of the eighteenth century enjoyed by Trowbridge and Bradford-on-Avon has eluded Melksham, but this bow-fronted house, now adjoining the transport depot in Spa Road, is of typical Regency style. The print is dated 1830 (the Church tower has not yet been moved, nor has the Town Hall been built).

THE FINE OLD REGENCY HOUSE is not what it was and now stands as a challenge to some competent restorer.

TWO VIEWS OF SPA ROAD from opposite directions. The attractive houses built alongside the bow-frontage have wrought iron balconies and were probably built around the time of the spa development.

The Spa, Melksham.

TWO VIEWS OF SPA ROAD before the First World War, in the vicinity of the three spa houses. Two features of these Edwardian photographs are the abundance of trees in the town and the paucity not only of traffic but also of people.

SPA ROAD, MELKSHAM.

SCOTLAND ROAD in around 1907. The houses were built by Spencers for the benefit of their workers and the road was so named by the manager, Mr Littlejohn Phillip, in a mood of nostalgia for his homeland. Margaret Street, which runs parallel, was named after his daughter. The viewer must imagine himself standing at the end of the road and facing Beanacre Road.

A FOOTBRIDGE AT THE END OF SCOTLAND ROAD was built to span the River Avon and thus give easier access to those employees of Spencers who lived in the forest area and who formerly had to take a walk through the town. A toll of $\frac{1}{2}d$. was payable, hence the name Halfpenny Bridge. The houses and the vacant land opposite were subsequently acquired by the Avon Rubber Company. The houses were let, and later sold, to Avon employees, and by the 1960s the Avon works buildings had spread up to the road and the river had been filled in at this point.

A VIEW FROM THE FRONT OF MELKSHAM HOUSE facing east. The two cottages built for the use of the groundsmen were demolished in favour of the Crown House development.

A VIEW OF THE ANCIENT TITHE BARN from the cricket field. It was converted for use as part of St Michael's School and now has been further converted to provide living accommodation.

MELKSHAM HOUSE FIRE

MELKSHAM HOUSE. There are records of a 'cottage' on this site in 1608. Various replacements and extensions continued over the years, particularly under the Long family who bought the premises in 1699. In the 1860s the grounds of Melksham House extended over what is now the cricket field and the cemetery right down to the river bank. A contemporary describes the area 'as more like a gentleman's park, beautifully timbered with limes, elms, chestnuts and one walnut tree near the river. In one spot there were five lovely elms. On Sunday evenings after divine service many people took their walks in the Conigre.' Today two lime trees survive. Conversion of Melksham House for use as a sports and social club for the employees of the Avon Rubber Company was carried out in 1920 and the formal opening of the club took place on Saturday 11 December. In the early hours of Wednesday 15 December a fire broke out which completely gutted the building. All that could be salvaged was the front of the house, which was preserved almost intact and today stands as before the fire. The house was rebuilt on lines more suited for a sports and social club than the original building was. The original rules of the club are surprising. The club was decreed by the company to be for the use of male employees only and an annual subscription of £1 was levied (the equivalent of £50 today) plus 5s. for each section joined.

THORNBANK HOUSE was pulled down and flats built on the site in the early 1970s. This was almost certainly taken pre-1914. Note the croquet hoops and what appears to be, for those days, an efficient lawnmower. At one time this was the home of Captain John Awdry, possibly the John Awdry in whose memory his son Sir John Awdry erected the reredos in the Parish Church in 1850.

THE START from outside the Unicorn Inn of an outing by wagonette in connection with the Baptist Church, apparently an all male event.

THE LACK OF NAVIGABLE RIVERS allied to the primitive road conditions prompted the construction of the Wilts. & Berks. Canal to run from Abingdon via Swindon (with branches to Chippenham and Calne) and Melksham to link with the Kennet & Avon Canal at Semington and thence to London or Bristol. The venture prospered initially, but by the 1880s the coming of the railway, together with the decline of the Somerset coalfields, marked the beginning of the end, and by 1898 the canal fell into disuse. It was closed by an Act of Parliament in 1914. Today in 1989 the line of the canal can easily be discerned through Melksham and on to Lacock.

THE SOUTHERN END of the Wilts. & Berks. Canal at the junction with the Kennet and Avon Canal at Semington, above. Below, the old line of the canal running up to the junction from Melksham. It is viewed from the point where the old GWR railway line to Devizes from Holt crossed the road.

THE LINE OF THE CANAL running between West End and Kenilworth Gardens.

A VIEW OF THE CANAL WHARF from the Spa Road bridge facing south. This stretch can be followed today between Kenilworth Gardens and West End (see previous view). The two warehouses seen in the photograph had corrugated iron roofs. Just after completion the sheds were being used for a political meeting at a General Election. Rival supporters threw stones on to the roof with such effect that the meeting had to be abandoned.

TWO VIEWS OF THE WHARF HOUSE. Above: when the canal was operative the wharf manager lived here. Below: the canal has been filled in. The house has now been demolished and a block of flats built on the site.

GALLOWS BRIDGE, which spanned the Wilts. & Berks. Canal, linked Stratton's Fields to those emerging into Spa Road and it stood where the junction of Pembroke Road and Lambourne Crescent now is. The reason for the name is a matter of conjecture. One legend suggests that a gallows once stood nearby before the canal was built. Another story is that a bargeman, standing at the rear of his barge as it passed under the bridge, caught his neck in a rope left dangling and was asphyxiated. It is possible that the name derives from a corruption of the word 'gallox', a name given to packhorse and cattle bridges. The bridge was finally demolished in 1913 as it was unsafe. The prominent tree was left standing in Lambourne Crescent until a few years ago.

PEMBROKE ROAD. Gallows Bridge was situated approximately where the car is parked.

A TRANQUIL SCENE on the Wilts. & Berks. Canal at Forest Lock. Traces of the lock are still visible off Methuen Avenue. The scene is of around 1910, before the abandonment of the canal in 1914. The cottage lasted until 1956 when it was demolished.

THE SITE OF THE OLD WHARF in the 1960s. Only the two corrugated iron sheds remain.

SANDRIDGE ROAD in around 1910.

FOREST ROAD looking towards Lacock. The houses on the left were mainly occupied by workers at Spencers and it was for their convenience that Murray Walk and the Halfpenny Bridge were developed.

THE CYCLE SHOP. Walter Gerrish started his cycle business in 1919. For years new cycles sold for £3 19s. 6d. (£3.98) and, for the luxury of a three-speed bicycle, £1 extra. At the outbreak of the Second World War his stock shed was full to the roof with new cycles, but within one week every one was sold. The building was dismantled in 1956.

THE TIMBER YARD. The local sawmills came into being in the early 1920s, instigated by Henry John Harding following the closure of the saw-pits. Sixteen men were employed felling oaks, ash, elm and walnut, the latter being used to make fitments for the RMS *Queen Mary* and *Queen Elizabeth*. Oak was also supplied for the Spanish railways. One tree felled was considered to be the finest in the country and it was exhibited at the Furnishing Trades Fair in London.

THE UNVEILING OF THE WAR MEMORIAL in 1919. One hundred and twenty-eight young men left the village to fight against Germany, twenty-three did not return. In the background to the left of the memorial the old village pound can be seen. This enclosure was dismantled in 1921 and its stone transported to the lord of the manor's home at Monkton Farleigh. The pound was put to good use; its function was to enclose stray animals from the Common and these would be released only when their owners paid the fine. A reference was made to the existence of a pound in the village as early as 1377.

THATCHED COTTAGE. This old cottage in Mill Lane, then Slippery Lane, was modernized in the '50s. In the great flood of 1935 the water reached a level halfway up its bedroom windows.

THE SLATE CLUB leaving the Bell Inn for their annual outing in Messrs Crook's charabancs of Melksham – note the solid tyres. In the late 1920s, the Bell Inn sold Oakhill Beers and Stout and Mr W. Hiscocks was the landlord.

WALTER GERRISH also ran the local taxi service and here you can see him in his new left-hand model T Ford. He then sold petrol out of two-gallon cans and if four gallons were sold in a week trade had been brisk. At a later date R.O.P. petrol was dispensed half a gallon at a time from a hand pump for 11*d*. per gallon.

ATWORTH, THE FORESTERS ARMS, an Ushers tied public house, viewed from the village market place. It is believed to have been an important sheep market in years gone by. The public house is now closed and the village gas-lamps have long since been replaced by electric ones.

ATWORTH, THE TOLL HOUSE, sometimes called Island House. This house looks much the same today, although a few years ago there were railings around the front of the house. Unfortunately these have been removed.

ATWORTH, THE CHURCH as it is today except that the yew trees are now much larger and the east window is now of stained glass depicting Jesus as a young man. It was made by Easton, who also constructed the Battle of Britain memorial window in Westminster Abbey.

THE CHURCH at Atworth taken from a watercolour by Buckler before it was pulled down. Only the tower remained and the church was rebuilt to a larger size to the south of the tower in around 1830. This has resulted in the grave of Mrs Jane Brown now being outside the church; it was she who founded the village charities.

THE GREEN, Atworth, outside a row of houses at one time called Pump Row. In this picture the pump is enclosed by a high stone wall which at a later date was reduced in height and railings added. The pump is unfortunately no longer present.

The Jubilee Clock, Atworth

ATWORTH VILLAGE TOWER CLOCK, built to celebrate the Diamond Jubilee of Queen Victoria. The road to the right has now been widened, the tree removed and a pavement put along the clock green. The milestone just visible is unfortunately now missing. Not showing, but on the sides of the clock are tablets added to commemorate the dead and those who served in the wars.

A TOWN HOUSE in a quiet country town? It is in fact the Cottage Hospital viewed from the Bath Road in 1906. The site for the hospital was given to the town by Mr George White of Whitley. He was a cheesemonger, operating in the sheds behind what is now the Assembly Hall. It was said that in his will he left three-quarters of a million pounds to the Church of England, perhaps worth ten million in today's money! He was a generous member of St Michael's Church and his gifts included the six stained glass windows in the clerestory.

LEAZE COTTAGE in Watson's Court, for many years the home of James Stratton and later of his three daughters: Mary, Maria and Caroline. Their brother George lived at The Giffords in Lowbourne and at one time it was possible to walk from Lowbourne to Spa Road without leaving Stratton territory.

Lowbourne House, Melksham.

LOWBOURNE HOUSE was built in around 1850. This was Dr Jasper Rumboll-Kings' house and later that of his nephew, Dr C.F. Rumboll, in whose memory the lych-gate at the entrance to the churchyard stands. The surgery was approached from the rear of the one-storey building. It was used during the last war to accommodate the Cottage Hospital staff. The grounds of Lowbourne House were extensive and ran across what is now Union Street down to Clacker's Brook. Union Street at that time was a cul-de-sac about half of its present length. In the 1860s there were three doctors in Melksham. In addition to Dr King, there were Dr Kendrick at Melksham House and Dr Plummer at Canon House in Canon Square.

MARTIGNY HOUSE in Spa Road, at the time of the photograph, the home of Mr E.J. Lee. The house still stands, but it is obscured behind the former offices of the Southern Electricity Board. Martigny Road derives its name from the existence of the house.

TWO VIEWS OF MESSRS TAYLOR'S CORN MILL which stood on the east side of the river bridge, having been converted from a woollen mill in 1793. The fire of 1873 gutted the mill. Horsemen were despatched to Devizes, Bradford and Trowbridge for fire engines to assist the Melksham brigade. With no possibility of saving the mill, efforts were directed to saving Matravers' cloth mill which was adjacent. The roof and floors of the mill fell in as did the wall facing the mill stream, causing burning wheat to tumble into the stream. This attracted hundreds of eels, which were caught and given to the voluntary helpers as a reward for their services. The mill was rebuilt but closed in 1939 when the premises were acquired by the Avon Rubber Company. The building still stands although reduced to two storeys.

A LATER VIEW of the corn mill, now taken over by the Avon. On the right is the grain silo built as an extension to Taylor's mill.

The Island, Melksham.   W 8660.

THIS HOUSE stood about in the middle of what is now the Avon employees' car park. It was the home of the Taylor family, the owners of the corn mill which can be glimpsed to the left. The house stood on an island created by the mainstream of the river on one side and the mill race and outflow on the other. This photograph dates from around the 1890s and was taken from the bridge.

A PRINT dated 1817 of the house near the bridge, now the offices of Avon Rubber Company. At this time the mill behind was run by J.L. Phillips who lived at Ark House. It seems likely that the house was leased separately from the mill. Certainly when Mr Matravers purchased the site, he lived in one of the houses at the rear of the large house. His son lived in the other one.

THE SAME HOUSE in the 1960s.

THE GRAIN SILO in process of being dismantled. The inner lining of the silo consisted of lengths of 4 × 4 timber bonded together by 6 in nails, a construction which defied normal demolition techniques and posed unexpected problems for the contractors.

A VIEW of the Avon works taken from what is now the King George playing fields. The tall building in the centre was the power house and on the left is the rear of what was Taylor's corn mill. The river diverged at this point, turning left over the weir and left again to pass under the bridge. In the 1960s the river was diverted to a new course nearer the playing fields and the old course filled in to provide extensions to the rubber works.

MELKSHAM WAS NOTORIOUS for its floods which were an annual hazard until the river was straightened in the 1960s. Both of these photographs were taken in 1926. Above is the King's Arms Hotel bus which met every train at the station to collect prospective guests. Below, the floods have abated somewhat. All of the houses on each side of the road have since disappeared. The house on the left included a boot and shoe shop run by Mr Percy Smith Keen.

FLOODS in 1950. The Gas Company offices are on the right with the manager's residence next door. This was later taken over by the Wiltshire Farmers.

MELKSHAM FLOODS were caused by a rise in level of the River Avon, but the worst in memory were caused by a cloudburst on an afternoon in May 1935. The downpour of about 45 minutes' duration was such that the Melksham to Holt bus was stranded all night at Broughton Gifford.

THE MELKSHAM RURAL DISTRICT COUNCIL HOUSING DEVELOPMENT at Dunch Road, taken over by the Urban District Council in 1934. Built in 1920 by Bigwood & Co. and in 1937 renamed Addison Road.

ST BARNABAS' CHURCH, Beanacre, in course of construction.

ST BARNABAS' CHURCH, opened in 1886, and below a triumphal arch built across the road in celebration.

OX ROASTING, above, on the occasion of Queen Victoria's Jubilee in 1897 and, below, at King George V's Coronation in 1911. The gentleman with the ladle in the top picture is Mr Hutton, a butcher, and in the lower picture is Mr Maurice Merrett whose descendants still live locally. The location of the upper picture is the Bear Field with Ark House among the trees. The lower picture is the Market Place with the former Branson's garage properties in the background, now part of the Crown House development.

THE DECLINE from Victorian and Edwardian gourmandising is perhaps reflected by the substitution of a pig for an ox at the time of Queen Elizabeth's Jubilee. The operator is still named Merrett, but not related to Maurice.

THE SALVATION ARMY FUNERAL PROCESSION for Mrs Annie Crook in Bath Road, 1912. This was said to be the last occasion that the band played at a funeral. Mrs Crook was the wife of Mr Joe Crook of Broughton Road; he was a pioneer in the hiring of charabancs.

THIS PICTURE was taken outside the Town Hall on the occasion of King George V's Jubilee. The figure perched rather precariously on top of the station wagon is said to have been the Jubilee Carnival Queen.

THE OPENING CEREMONY of the pavilion on King George playing fields in 1910, when it was not in fact a public playing field, but the headquarters of the Melksham Cricket Club. Lowbourne School used to hold its annual sports on the field with the competitors marching past the VIP guests and School Governors before the events began, saluting with the raised right arm. The salute was discontinued in 1935!

A VIEW FROM THE CHURCH TOWER looking down on the old Vicarage gardens.

THE AVON VALE HUNT meeting outside the King's Arms Hotel. This was a favourite meeting place at the start of the century when the then Duke of Beaufort was a regular follower. Note the monkey puzzle tree outside Clare House: this was for many years a feature of the Market Place.

TWO GROUPS OF WORKERS in the Avon Rubber Works. Above, from the extruding department, with the foreman Arthur Sleightholme. Below, girls from the open cure department. George Comley the foreman is on the extreme right.

AVON RUBBER COMPANY OFFICE STAFF, probably the accounts department. Left to right: Miss Chandler, Mr P. Rebbeck, Mr W. Chatworthy, Mr R. Snook, Miss Davis, Mr Percy Hughes, Miss Boot. The date, 1920, is mistaken since Roly Snook, who is still with us, has identified the personnel and he was born in 1900.

A TENNIS PARTY comprising Avon personnel, with Major Fuller in the chair. The location and date are unidentified.

EMPLOYEES AT MAGGS' MATTING FACTORY protesting against the use of 'Chinese slave labour'. There was, however, no intention on the part of Mr Charles Maggs to introduce Chinese labour at Melksham. At the General Election in January 1906 the Liberal Party was making an issue of Tory proposals to introduce Chinese labour in South African mines. Sir John Fuller, the Liberal candidate, held his eve of poll meeting in the Melksham Town Hall and proceedings were enlivened by the appearance on the platform of the four bewigged and enchained protesters.

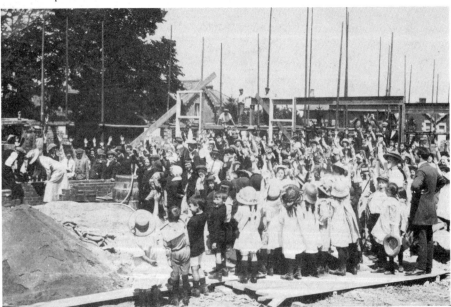

LAYING OF THE FOUNDATION STONE at Lowbourne School in 1909.

A GROUP OF EMPLOYEES of the Avon Rubber Company taken in around 1930 at Melksham House. The managing director, Major R.F. Fuller, is seated centre and on his right Mr O.F. Swanborough, the works' manager and, subsequently, managing director.

AVON RUBBER COMPANY – the Joint Works Council of around 1950. The front row from right to left are: Roy Gee, Frank Wilkins, Frank Featherstone, F Kendall-Jones, O.F. Swanborough, George Bailey and W. Cliffe.

CHARLES MAGGS and a group of his employees at the ropeworks taken sometime in the 1890s.

MR GURNEY OF LONDON built this steam coach and set off on a maiden journey to Bath in 1829. When he arrived in Melksham the Annual Fair was in progress and he was met by a hostile mob throwing stones at the vehicle and threatening the passengers. A safe refuge was found for the coach and the ladies and gentlemen of the party were lodged overnight in the King's Arms. When the demonstrators gathered early next morning they found that their quarry had already left. The Duke of Wellington was one of the passengers on the trip.

A MEETING OF THE PRIMROSE LEAGUE at The Chestnuts, Bath Road, in c. 1910. Note the open countryside behind, now engulfed by the Avon factory.

AN EDWARDIAN WEDDING GROUP, published here in the hope that someone may identify the occasion and/or the place.

A GROUP at the opening of the new St Michael's Junior School at Queensway in the 1960s. Left to right are: Mr Saunders (Headmaster), Mr D. Aust (Churchwarden) Revd Michael Newman, Mrs Saunders, Canon Cyril Witcomb, Mr R.F. Bush (Chairman, Melksham UDC). The gentleman on the right has yet to be identified.

THE CLERGY OF ST MICHAEL'S CHURCH in the 1930s. Left to right are: Revd Webster and Revd Phillips, Canon Sangster (Vicar) and Revd Barry.

A FAREWELL PRESENTATION to Canon Basil Aston, DSO, vicar of Melksham. The presentation is being made by Mr D. Aust (vicar's warden). On the extreme left is Mr Jack Arlott (organist and choirmaster) and on the right Mr Mervyn Hawkes (people's warden).

MRS ASTON'S BIBLE CLASS 1929. Jesse Coleman is third from left, second row. George Webb is third from left, third row. In the back row, Francis Wilkins, then and into old age inseparable from his cap.

ST MICHAEL'S CHURCH CHOIR sometime before 1914, surely the heyday of the Anglican Church. The organist and choirmaster was Jimmy Ogle (the diminutive figure, fifth from the left, standing). The boys alone met for practice two evenings a week in Mr Ogle's drawing room at Canon House with Mrs Ogle sitting at the rear prepared to administer a box around the ear to any boy lapsing in musicianship or behaviour.

THE PARISH CHURCH BELLS. There were six bells in the old tower which was moved to the west end of the church in 1845. These bells had been cast in 1703. They were rehung and quarter turned in 1896 when two new bells were added. The bells were grounded for further maintenance in 1910, when this picture was taken. From left to right: Mr Sartain, Mr Aust, Mr Archard, Dr Rumboll, Mr Bloomfield, Mr Burbidge, Mr Angell, Revd Basil Aston, Mr Angel.

MISS MARIA STRATTON on her tricycle in 1910 at the age of 59. While the other Melksham Strattons left the Church of England for the Methodists or Congregationalists, she continued a devout Anglican, particularly at the church at Beanacre with her tricycle, which was her only means of transport. An outspoken and domineering woman, in addition to playing the harmonium she called the tune in running St Barnabas', with the curate as a supernumerary.

MISS MARIA STRATTON'S BIBLE CLASS in 1890. Presumably Miss Stratton is the lady in the striped dress standing in the centre. Her great nephew, John Stratton, writes that she ran a bible class for men at Leaze Cottage where she lived until 1925. This appears to be something different with men, women and children.

MISS CAROLINE STRATTON, Maria's sister, joined the Congregationalists and her chief contribution was running the men's bible class. She lived at Leaze Cottage and died in 1949. She enjoys a unique distinction in that she is buried in the same grave as her sister Charlotte, who died 102 years earlier.

MR SALTER on his three-wheeler in the Market Place. This foot-propelled vehicle is described as an invalid carriage, although it would appear to need a fairly fit invalid to operate those foot treadles.

THE DIRECTORS of the Wilts. Somerset and Weymouth Railway Company made an experimental trip from Bath to Melksham via Thingley Junction on 7 September 1848. At Melksham Station the tram was received 'with loud cheering from the assembled populace'. In this picture the lines are being changed from Brunel's broad gauge to the narrower gauge then in general use. Note the Victorian dresses and the advertisements for steamship trips to America. The date here was 1874.

A PRESENTATION to the retiring station master, Mr Sealy, in the 1950s. At this distance in time it is surprising to see how large a staff was involved (four of the company can be identified as visitors). There was, in fact, a staff of 60.

MELKSHAM GWR

TWO VIEWS OF MELKSHAM STATION, one in its heyday, the other in the process of demolition after closure under the Beeching plan in the 1960s. It was re-opened for limited passenger service in the 1980s.

LITTLE IS KNOWN OF THIS MELKSHAM TOWN BAND although the uniforms suggest the 1890s. The location is identified as in the fields at the rear of Conigre Farm, known locally as The Conigre.

THE MELKSHAM CORONATION SILVER BAND, raised and equipped in 1937. A number of the musicians still live in the area today. The bare-headed secretary on the left is Arthur Hillier, with Major C.W. Maggs (president) and Percy Hughes (chairman) on the right of the bass drum. The band lapsed during the Second World War and attempts to reform after 1946 failed.

THE OPENING CEREMONY of the new works canteen at the Avon in the early 1940s. Major Robert and Mrs Fuller are in the doorway.

AFTER THE OPENING, Mrs Fuller serves the first cup of tea to Mr R.F. Comley (sales director). Behind him are Mr Frank Featherstone (employment manager), Mr Lovell (company secretary), Mr Cliffe (works engineer) and Mr Jack Roberts (chief draughtsman).

THE DUKE OF EDINBURGH visited the Avon in 1960 after landing by helicopter on the factory car park. He was met by Mr H. Floyd (chairman) and Mr O.F. Swanborough (managing director).

QUEEN MARY visited the Avon during the First World War and is here photographed with a group of employees, with Major Fuller on her right and Mr Swanborough on her left.

'LITTLE' JOHN CHAPMAN, a Melksham character, who died in the 1920s aged 68. The location is Crook's shop, which stood roughly where the Avon works entrance is nowadays. He attributed his stature to the fact that when he was a boy 'he was a good 'un' and received so many pats on the head that it stunted his growth'.

BY CONTRAST Fred Kempster, born at Seend, who according to the *Guinness Book of Records* was 8 ft 4½ in tall, though photographic evidence suggests less. This picture was taken outside the King's Arms during the First World War. Kempster capitalized on his appearance by engaging a manager and undertaking several tours during which, in Germany, he is reported to have married a girl almost as tall as himself. The gentleman in the bowler hat is variously held to be either his manager or the then landlord of the King's Arms.

The inscription reads:

THIS SPECIMEN OF THE
BOS PRIMIGENIUS,
WAS FOUND IN THE BED OF THE RIVER, AT MELKSHAM,
IN THE YEAR 1838, AND WAS PURCHASED BY SUBSCRIP-
-TION FROM THE EXECUTORS OF J.L.PHILLIPS, ESQ^{RE}
AND PLACED IN THIS ROOM FOR SAFETY,
BY PERMISSION OF
THE MELKSHAM MARKET COMPANY, A·D 1856.

SOME FISHERMEN USING A NET in a deep pool in the Avon just below the Vicarage drew up the horns and part of the skull of an ox in May 1838. It was proved to be part of a fossil skull of an ox believed to be of the Palaeolithic era. The specimen, suitably mounted, hangs over the door of the Main Hall in the Town Hall. In the late 1970s a number of iron and bronze objects were recovered from the River Avon. These were identified as spear heads, part of a rapier and three phalerae (bronze discs presumed to have some decorative function). Some of these are British but others are exotic pieces from Europe and are dated around 600 BC.

A CONGREGATIONAL SUNDAY SCHOOL FESTIVAL outside the New Hall in around 1886.

THE AVON SPORTS & SOCIAL CLUB RUGBY FOOTBALL SECTION 1930. Back row: F. Hillman, –?–, G. Scott, F. Pickston, R. Love, –?–, E. Dix, ? Hartland, A.E. Hewes. Second row: S. Haddelton, K. Sterry, K.W. Merrett, H.G. Gunstone, S. Hewes, M. Haddrell, D. Bullock, A. Clark, S. Tyndale. Seated: D. Bennett, F. Harding, D. Brown, C. Welham, A. Gale, D. Rigby, –?–, D. Uncles, –?–. Front row: C. Harrell, F. England, G. Bryant, C. Hartland.

MELKSHAM & AVON UNITED FOOTBALL CLUB 1920. Back row: L. Mitcham, J. Dicks, O. Newman, F. Dicks, G.H. Davis, J.F. Lawrence. Middle row: H. Taylor, O. Marchant, B. Lewington, H. Dodimead, F. Hudd, Capt. Mortimer, F. Radford. Seated: W. Ponting, S. Ponting, Major Fuller, W.E. Rodford, J. Missen, C. Carnell.

THE CO-OPERATIVE WHOLESALE SOCIETY established a creamery south of the station in 1920 and collected milk from the surrounding countryside. With a capacity to handle many thousands of gallons daily it employed 30–40 hands.

THE ARK FIELDS in around 1955, before the Western Way was built and the river straightened.

AN AERIAL VIEW of Old Broughton Road at its junction with Bath Road. Probably taken in the late 1940s. The Avon canteen is there and the cottages on the other side of the works' entrance are still there, as are the row of three houses and a shop opposite the Unicorn.

TAKEN AT THE SAME TIME as the above picture, but from a higher view point and therefore giving an extended view of the works. Note the Halfpenny Bridge and Murray Walk. The river runs along the edge of the factory; it was later to be diverted almost to the boundary hedge of the adjoining fields.

DECORATIONS IN THE HIGH STREET in 1874 to celebrate the wedding of Prince Alfred, Duke of Edinburgh, the second son of Queen Victoria, to Princess Marie. She was the only daughter of the Tsar of Russia. The building on the left is Stratton, Son and Mead's.

THE SAME SCENE as above, but viewed from the opposite direction. The gabled building in the centre is now D.J. Hiam's, once the site of stables. At the time of this photograph it was a baker's. Later it became a fishmonger's, before being acquired by W.H. Smith & Sons. The trees behind the archway are perhaps the same linden trees we have seen in photographs of a later date.

ACKNOWLEDGEMENTS

In compiling this collection I have been indebted to the following for their assistance:

Mr P.A.J. Brown for permission to quote from the transcript of William Bolwell's reminiscences, for information based on his own knowledge of the town and for permission to draw on his collection of old photographs. Mr David Webb and Mr Derek Gerrish for the items relating to Atworth and Broughton Gifford respectively. Mr Aubrey Winter, Mr Sidney Bell, Mr and Mrs Donald Watts and Mrs Isabel Ide for information and Mr N.W.G. Cole for the loan of photographs. Mr Colin Venton for permission to quote from Miss Vernon's preface to the *Guide to Melksham* published by Mr Venton in 1966. Mr Vincent Seears whose correspondence with the late Mr George Davis is an invaluable source of information. Lt. Commander B.S. Mudge and Mrs Linda Maslen who typed the scripts.